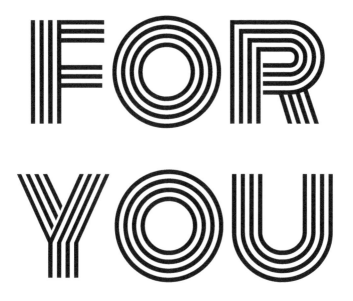

FOR YOU

Krystel Fortis

For You
Written by Krystel Fortis

All rights reserved.

CONTENTS
(MESSY)

PLAYLIST

Circles — Post Malone
Sober — Demi Lovato
Beautiful People — Ed Sheeran
Lose You to Love Me — Selena Gomez
Make it With You — Bread
Fuel on the Fire — Bear's Den
i love you — Billie Eilish
Rush — Lewis Capaldi
Lost Without You — Freya Ridings
Paperweight — Joshua Radin
Let's Fall in Love for the Night — Finneas
All I Ask — Adele
Beast of Burden — Rolling Stones
Audition — Emma Stone
Boston — Dermot Kennedy
Burning House — Cam
Don't Know Why — Norah Jones

PLAYLIST

Like a Wrecking Ball — Eric Church

Tennessee Whiskey — Chris Stapelton

Whiskey and Morphine — Alexander Jean

Ocean Eyes — Billie Eilish

If the World Was Ending — JP Saxe

Surrender — Natalie Taylor

Just You and I — Tom Walker

Trouble (Stripped) — Halsey

Me & Mr Jones — Amy Winehouse

Everything I Wanted — Billie Eilish

Gravity — Sara Bareilles

Don't Let Her — Walker Hayes

Medicine — Daughter

Drinkin' too Much (8pm) — Sam Hunt

Let Me Go — Hailee Steinfeld

Be Alright — Dean Lewis

I'll Never Love Again — Lady Gaga

Bundle of Joy — Benny Martin

INTRODUCTION

I can't quite put a smell to one of the happiest places I know. Probably because it smells like you. But god, can I feel it. My breath gets deeper and deeper and tears start to form behind my eyes. I can feel the fight against them coming on strong already and I haven't even walked in yet. Honestly just standing in front of this beautiful place is enough. I can tell you who's sitting at the bar and what sassy remark Roxy is making at someone. I can see the lights and how dim they are. Just never dim enough for the darkest corners of what we will do inside. I can see the tall bar top tables across the room and the way the balls are tossed randomly across the pool table. So I open the door and walk in. I'm home.

The one place that knows me at my very worst and best all in the same night, sometimes. Instantly a smile finds my face. I scan across to see which booth it'll be tonight. Which one will be the lucky one. Always a little shy and nervous at the bar wondering who is listening to us order. But who fucking cares because you always tie me in closer to the bar as you wrap one arm around me to place both your hands on the bar. The simplest questions about the current IPAs knowing full well what both of us are ordering always. A sly comment about the double pour and a quick reminder about "regular not diet" and we are off. Being pushed into the roughest booth seats that have been ripped for years now but being the most comfortable I've ever felt between a flannel and a cold wall.

The first few sips always have me questioning what kind of night it will be. God, if they would just turn down the lights a little more. If we get up now to put on the right music you know how this evening will end. Words getting thrown back and forth and honestly I have already forgotten there are others sitting around us, much less anywhere else in the room. My mind is open now and I can feel everything. The music, the drunk running down inside of me.

The sudden and desperate urge to run to the restroom hits. Oh that bathroom has seen my drunkenness. The mirrors always seem foggy but more likely that's just my eyes after the 3 rum and cokes I've had, that usually amount to about 6. The bathroom stalls get all my sloppiness, as I believe I can "get it all out" while I'm in there. I wipe off the excess eyeliner that naturally starts to fade as the night gets darker. Then I quickly pull it together to walk back out confidently, smirking, knowing that the bathroom and I have a special bond that no one else knows about.

I know now that the moment has come where we are about to get even sillier than before. Whether it be the feel of your socks underneath the high tops while we take sips between darts. Or the ridiculous words we will write on whatever we can find or the words that start to create stories. This place. It's magic, I tell you. There's nothing quite like it. In these moments I am completely detached from any form of reality. There is no world outside of this dingy dive. My happiness lives here, in this place, in this moment. It has seen tears and first kisses and drunkenness and breakups and fights and stories and dances and lives. The decision to close out is always something close to my heart because it's one last moment with my bartender, my friend, if only for the night. She sees our story. My story. But she pretends not to. It's all just a glimpse in her perspective, anyway. No one could ever truly know what this place means to me. What it has given me over and over and what it has done to change me. I walk out and a little piece of me is left behind in that bar for another time. I can feel it the moment the door closes behind me. It's like I'm still there, in that moment. And it's always pulling me back.

The parking lot has seen our worried plans to get out of there and what the night might bring after. If only I could just relive the night we laid in the street. The concrete was so cold on my back but I wasn't focused. Every time I go back I think about it. It wasn't just any busy street. It was Gilly's street front. The street front that has had me pressed against the closed down stores during phone calls and make out sessions. The street that has led me down side roads for nights you only talk about in third person.

There is probably so much more I have left out but for tonight, this will do. Just like my bar, my place, my home.

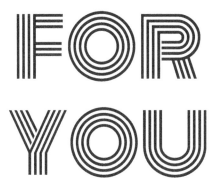

FOR YOU

Krystel Fortis

For You

LOVE YOU

~~Ducking Drink~~ Autocorrect
F   u

I miss your calm so much.

Your patience and frustration

all wrapped in one.

The way you hated and loved

every last thing about me.

If only the worst of all of this

was the way you were trying so

desperately to figure me out.

whole FOODS, and Houston's and

Jesus please take the wheel to the freeway.

I'm headed to pick up that one word you need to hear me say over and over.

I'm learning to love Gin because you don't exist in that drunk.

I'll just allow autocorrect to have it this time.

Just like every ducking time before.

Things are better this way.

All We Needed

The dimmed lights, neon, and

drinks could romance even the

coldest of souls.

This is where they found lust

and themselves.

Without a doubt, this place could

always be found on a napkin or

tattered notebook.

This is what I'm sure a warm &

loving home must feel like, but I

couldn't tell you for sure.

But that's what it felt like to us.

The truths existed in the dark booth corners and in barefoot dart matches.

The idea that the bartend knew more about us than any other person alive, had to count for something.

Water rings still wet all over the

table as a symbol of how well

the evening is going.

If there was a way to bottle up

those nights, you wouldn't be able

to put a price tag on them.

Sometimes it felt like all they

were was booze soaked nights.

And that was all they needed to

be.

One Day

One day we are finally us.

You & Me

Happy, in love, desperately

obsessed and helping build each

other.

Why can't we have it all, will be

our motto.

Sunsets and lakes and front

porch summer nights and dark

dives and comfy pajama pants, I

make you wear.

Kissing me in the kitchen and

premiers we fly into the city for

and trips with so many stories

for lifetimes ahead.

One day...

We will walk on gravel streets

with green rolling hills to our

right and left.

A pub with live music and

whiskey shots with our beer.

Midnights will be filled with
scattered notebooks, laptops,
naked toes, creation, and
cigarette breaks (that I'll
forever hate).

One day...

You'll talk to my belly and
promise you'll give it the world no
matter what it takes.

You'll introduce them to Baby &
Papa bear and we will all sit

back and watch them

learn the light and darkness the

world has to offer.

One day...

Ink to paper

It fades and then comes back

strong.

A beautiful bleed it has left

behind.

You have to really want it

because of how much time it

takes to get it right.

It's just like you and me.

Maybe after years of practice,

we could get it right too.

Thank you Boston, time and time again, thank you.

Water In My Whiskey

A little watered down whiskey

and pandora reminding me why

I've converted to audible books

and podcasts lately.

Productivity is my new favorite

distraction.

Funny to think that you hated

how type A I was before.

You'd absolutely hate me now.

I don't really write anymore.

Until some chord is struck.

Last night's lesson taught me to listen to my heart.

"Your heart will always know what you desire before your mind does."

Did you know that according to this lesson, our hearts believe in the impossible and if we just let it, we can have the impossible?

Do you think that's true?

I guess that was the chord I
needed to get on here today.

We Are Art

You and I are the simplest version of art, nature ever created.

We are and because of it, there is a little more light in the universe.

I wish we could save those weaker, the way you save me daily.

We could show them how far the

wrong path will get you, if they

would give us the chance.

Don't let these words scare you,

Babe, like unhealthy and

addiction.

We are the dream they're all

scared of having.

'Til the End

Do whatever the hell you want...

As long as every single second of

it is with me.

I miss you already and youre

sitting right fucking next to me.

I cant live without you,

actually,

at all.

Nothing on this road scares me

except not knowing whether you'll

be with me until the very end.

Please just be with me wherever

this path may lead.

Give us this Moon

Give us this moon, our nightly

muse

While the world loses all its

senses,

we become the wiser.

Let it lead the way through our

darkest moments and always be

our guide back to one another.

Give us this moon, our nightly

muse for each drenched and

darkened path on its surface

reminds us of the dreams we

share.

Childhood fantasies turned

adulthood creative.

For out there, in the darkness,

hides our infinite, spitfire

romance.

We are here to revel and survive

in its power.

Give us this moon, our nightly

muse.

We Are

We are who I've always wanted

to be.

Laughs and stories.

Creativity and past.

And passion rolled into one.

I Miss... You

I could make you think twice if

I just licked your lip a little

longer.

Make me wet....

It's been so fucking long since I've

felt that way.

Maybe that is the root of all of

it.

The passion is gone.

It is what drove me to be me

and now it's gone and so am I.

I long for the kind of days that

take you up a hill off to a

corner to shove your fingers up

my skirt until I scream.

I fucking miss the days that I

considered letting you shove me

onto a dirty bar bathroom sink.

Feel stupid and giddy and not

stop blushing.

Have me thinking about

everything you're going to do to me

if only I could spare a few

minutes to see you and I'd take

it.

The pictures of rulers on wooden

dining room tables and a dim

night stand light that give the

welts across my ass your

favorite shade of red.

I was going crazy thinking of

any place I could send you dirty

pictures in half hidden hotel

hallways.

Just to make you feel a little

wild and hard from whatever

distance.

I don't even talk like this

anymore.

I haven't dreamt about being

tied up to my bed posts for

months now.

I can still feel the heat that

made me pull off the road just

to tell you exactly how I wanted

to lick the tip of you to fruition.

You must think about the night

my hands left prints on the

back of the car and how good

it felt to have the neighborhood

see you take me the way you

wanted.

How could you not.

I can't ever forget the spanking

and sting I felt for 2 days after.

Nothing has ever had me more

intrigued.

I'm losing my steam.

I don't even see myself anymore

in the mirror.

That woman you used to have.

She's gone.

I know because I used to see her

and feel her coming out of my

pores. That feeling is like nothing

else. It makes me breathe a

certain way and moves my lips

along with my tongue and teeth.

A smirk that hasn't seen my

face since you aren't around.

I would get wet at the thought of

you.

At the scent leaving a page.

How bad you wanted me if not

for anything but the way my

finger left your hand.

For You

Now that I have your attention

For You

Wonderland

Rescue me from this fucking hell.

Take me away with you to

wonderland.

A world filled with dark dives

and sake shots.

Where purple hours never last

long enough and you'll remember

every sentence I've ever uttered.

Give me so much to write about

that I can't spend another

~~Ducking~~ second typing
f
in that "girly" looking text.

Lets laugh our asses off all the

way to our drunken stupor and

be the only high I'll ever need.

Keep loving me to safety for all

the days of our lives and be my

hero on nights I have to buy a

parking pass.

So take me now your

wonderland awaits today and

always, all ways.

Big Buzz

Driving home with a buzz big

enough for the music to take

over my mind.

You are it for me.

You always will be.

You are my Fuel on the Fire.

So, let's build our own Bear's

Den.

A home I won't drive away from

ever.

I don't need anything perfect and

I never have.

Truth is...

I've always only wanted you in

all the ways that make you

real...

Tangible.

It seems you've become more my

man in every second of our days.

You're everything I ever dreamt

you were.

My ears are ringing and I'm typing without looking at the screen.

I can hear you say "did you just finish writing a book?"

Like you believe I'm capable of writing novels effortlessly.

I hope I live up to all you believe me to be.

I want to be all of that and more.

And maybe I am now, because

of you.

I'll just be here in this moment,

letting the music fill not only my

car, but also my

soul and thinking and dreaming

of all that we have become and

will be.

And...

Run Away

Run away with me.

Let's not tell a damn soul.

Let us build a dream world
together.

Let them wonder in complete
confusion.

Let's live in mornings of deep
conversation over coffee.

Late night dive bars with darts
and pool tables.

We need to be drunk on us, all

day, every day, forever.

K. Fortis

For You

Breathe Beautiful

Sometimes passion is worth

destruction

For You

YOU'RE SORRY

Radio Silence

I want to believe it was all in

my head.

That you never truly loved me.

That you couldn't possibly care.

That the radio silence is the

truth.

But how can I?

You promised me, page after page

that no matter what reality

looked like that you would

forever exist in the fantasy with

me.

I'm going to put it in the mail

and remind you.

Remind you what it felt like the

day I met your dancing fool side.

Remind you of how it felt to see

your heart fall onto the table

from light years away.

Remind you of the feel of the

darker floors beneath your feet

with only socks on.

Remind you how we ran the

world.

How drinks could taste like

people and how my heart will

never belong to anyone but you.

So how could I believe it to be

all in my head when I can still

feel it in my heart?

How Dare You

You put this on me?

"If you continue to love me this way then I'll become better, probably."

As though my efforts were required in order to receive what I already deserved.

So I loved harder, and gave more of me, and wept myself to sleep at night.

I wrote for you and I worked for
you and I paid for you and
destroyed myself for you.

More and more, everyday, I lost
pieces of me... for you.

And then without a mere thank
you, you left.

Dissolved into thin air.

You took my compassion and
empathy and knowledge with you

and left without a crumb trail

behind.

How dare you.

Title Me

You will forever see me the way

you choose to see me.

Use me as your excuse.

Your way to feel better.

Your way to be better.

For fucks sake let me be the

scapegoat.

The flighty.

The irresponsible.

The bitchy.

The confrontational.

The demeaning.

The controlling.

The judge mental.

The opinionated.

The unfiltered.

Pick and choose.... so many to

pick from.

Let me be whatever you'll have

me to be...

But dear god, don't you dare see

me as,

The confident.

The upright.

The healer.

The truth teller.

The raw.

The real.

The lover.

The fighter....

No please.

Choose for me a title if you will.

A Letter to you,

Maybe it's because I want
to be single.
Maybe it's because I have
men throwing themselves at
me. Maybe it's because there
might be someone better.
There are a million maybes
but the reasons I know are
seemingly endless.

You need to get a job. You
need to have goals to create
the dreams you want.
Goals are not just thoughts.
They are plans written in
stone that you stick to and
accomplish. You need to
learn to be considerate of
your family and friends.

Stop thinking everyone is fine just because they say they are. You are floating around Los Angeles without a plan while your family deals with the hard parts. You have nothing to do. You could help instead of hurt. You could offer sometimes. Just in every instance. You need to stop spending if you don't have the means.

It's the eating out, drinking, vacations, entertainment, schmoozing friends, and everything else. Retirement accounts aren't for spending. That isn't even yours to spend.

You need to go to therapy to work through your problems. You need to work through your denial. Your denial of childhood abuse. Your denial of the way your life is really being lived. Your denial about who you are. Your denial about your age. You need to work through your jealousy. The jealousy that throws you into a crazy internal rage that makes you do the most hurtful things. You create competitions in your mind instead of being able to have open honest communication. You need to learn how to have honest conversation. Conversation that isn't always happy and perfect. That may teach you a thing or two. Being open to seeing another side other than your own. The potential of being wrong or proved right but having a full discussion to get to that point.

You need to learn how to set priorities. Studying for 150 hours a week is bull and we all know it. Priorities need to be set based on what is actually important, not just the things you like doing. You need to stop faking everything. Pretending to be amazing isn't helping you or anyone around you.

It's hurting everyone.

You have a major issue with denial. You could deny that the sky is blue if you wanted to be right about something to make yourself feel better. Everything isn't an attack and you need to find out why you feel that way so often. What makes you feel that people are always trying to prove you wrong. Maybe if you weren't faking so much of your existence you wouldn't feel the need to defend lies. You pretend to be all these things. A writer and producer and hard working and a romantic. The list goes on. It's not enough to "know" you need to change these things. You are 45. Enough is enough and honestly I've had enough.

You have convinced me time and time again that things are different and better and going to be incredible and the sad part is I know eventually out of pure dumb luck you will make it. Honestly because you were gifted an incredible talent that you don't even appreciate enough to work hard for.

But inevitably someone will bump into you by accident

and make your dreams
come true. And at the
moment I will be sad and
mad and jealous that people
like you get what you never
worked for.

As for me, I can't. I put
myself into this. Into you. I
believe in you and want the
best for you. But I can't be
the only one out of the two
of us who cares to try and
who gets knocked down for
it. You always make me feel
small and the fact is that
you are small. So much
smaller than me. You could
be a giant but you won't be.
You refuse to be. I want you
to just care for once about

what I am telling you. This
isn't "just one persons opinion".
This is just the one person
willing to tell you. You deserve

love and honestly I want to
be that person for you but I
refuse to lose myself in that
process. I refuse to be your
excuse this time. You always
give me back my writer's
touch and for that I am
forever grateful. You made
me believe in romance again.
Your mind and stories make
me happy. You always show
my son love when you are
around and for that I know
he will always love you.
I wish I didn't have to say
these things because I know

they will hurt. They have to because if they don't then you still won't believe them. Maybe one day you will believe me instead of telling me I'm wrong or that I think I know what I don't. And maybe then you will fix them but for now I'm not sure if I believe everyone and anyone can truly change anymore. Maybe some people just can't. Maybe some of us are creatures of habit who can not see the light they were given and don't want to believe there is a future better than what they know.

Love you always,
K. Fortis

K. Fortis

For You

Back to our regularly scheduled

program...

For You

Questions

My doubt has creeped in again
and for the moment I think I
should run away from us... as
far as possible.

Questions shooting at me from all
directions.

Questions with answers I know
all too well and choose not to
accept.

We've been here before and I

have no doubt we will be here

again soon.

For we have always been just

this.

A hope of a future.

A false reality you desperately

want to provide me.

At the end of the day you still

head home for a break from

our fantasy and I sink.

I Know this moment all too well.

You will always be you and I
will always be me.

There's only so many ways we
can pretend to be something else.

Another false promise of your
desire to help and God I know
you believe it to your core.

I just know below even the
deepest parts of you, remains a
truth.

That truth and I have never

seen eye to eye.

I will always be too much and too little, and you will never be enough, and everything I've ever wanted.

Codependency

I sat back and watched as he tried to hide the discomfort that was bubbling to the surface.

He was so deeply pained but couldn't put words or actions to it.

I'm not even sure if he was completely aware of it or if it had just been this way his whole life.

With every glance I tried to

reach him at his core.

I tried to show him I was there,

in him, holding all the shattered

pieces.

Just waiting for him to tell me

he wanted them put back

together.

He could see me but he couldn't

feel me.

He was unsure, not only of me,

but also what he would do if he

was whole again.

I sat back, torn between

releasing him in hopes he would

find another to repair his

wounds and

staying until I knew he would be

ok.

Your Real Life Fantasy

You wanted to tell me everything,

but you couldn't.

You wanted to collapse in my

arms, but you wouldn't allow

yourself.

But you cared about me, almost

effortlessly.

Worrying about me came so

natural, you had to fight the

urges to rush to me.

You were so guarded.

Not just with me but with

everyone.

Did anyone really know you or

how you felt?

I have had so few, honest, to the

core conversations with you.

I could count them on one hand.

In those moments there was

nothing stopping me from being in

complete awe of you and it was

all I longed for every other

moment I spent with you.

But that wasn't where you felt

safe.

Not in those heart and soul

filled connections.

Instead safety comes in partially

removed fictional stories.

The tragic fairy tales you saw

yourself in.

K. Fortis

For You

I'M SORRY

Sorry

I am sorry.

Sorry that I can't remember the

days

I hurt you the worst.

The moments that have both

made and shattered you.

I apologize for being both the

Kryptonite and

poison you never deserved.

I hate to have to be the one

that builds you back up from

the brokenness I created.

I am so sorry that I have been

the heartbreak in your love

story instead of

the magical romance you have

always deserved.

I wish I could turn back time

and give you the softest of

landings and make sure you

Knew every second of everyday
that you were too good for me.
I love you and yet I am the one
who has crushed you.
What can I say about love if I
have been more of Hades than
heaven in your world?
It makes me tear up at the
thought of me ripping you apart.
I hate that I have caused any
moments of pain in your life.
I am sorry.

You Should Know

Every part of me wants to be your muse and happy place and life's desire and yet I sat there today in awe at the stories you told.

I felt so foolish to be dumbfounded at the thought.

I hate that I can't even remember some of the most defining moments.

I wish I could exchange every memory of your pain for only the pleasures that rest within me.

If I could destroy every hurtful thing I ever did or said to you, I would in a heartbeat.

I felt like I should walk away today.

Knowing you deserve much much more than me.

You deserve only the most

romantic life.

A world of creation and passion

and lust and love and happiness

and everything you've ever

dreamt of.

I just wanted you to know.

Codependency part 2

Let me be your stronger half

and show you all the things

you've never let yourself feel.

Allow my empathy to seep

through your heart and soul.

I can teach you how to connect

to your softer side because I see

your strengths.

I see all your strengths.

Your excuses appear in your eyes

before they are spoken.

So let me alleviate your fears.

I have always believed in you.

You see a forest of regret and

failures but my eyes are affixed

on that shadow of

hope behind it all.

You can't hide this from me.

My frustration arises as you

choose to believe deeper in your

demise than your dreams and

destiny.

I can only love you for the things

I know you are meant to be.

Maybe this is my fault.

Once I have shown you your

path, I need to move onto the

next.

My fate is eternal loneliness

because I was placed here only

for your growth.

Please go out into this world with

the confidence I have in you.

You don't need to believe in you,

just believe in me and all that I

know you are.

I will always love you, all ways.

Run

I need to run away.

To leave you to your destiny

because I am your downfall.

I have become all your dreams,

aspirations, and heartache.

You need me more than you don't

and you can't have me because

I was born to destroy you.

I am here to make you believe in

the impossible.

And you should believe that with

every last ounce of who you are.

In reality, I mean outside of our

world, you can't be all that you

were meant to be if I stay.

With me here, you will never

dream bigger than me.

And believe me when I say I am

not the sun, moon and stars, not

for you.

You are so much more than me.

You will see, the minute I stage

my disappearance, how much

more you were made to be.

You may think you love who you

are with me.

The man I make you.

But the truth is, you are nothing

with me.

I break apart your life without

you noticing.

You could never have been what

you were meant to be without
me.

You needed me to show you but I
can't keep you.

You need to refocus that passion
into something the world needs.

Something I need you to be.

The man I have always known
you to be.

I will watch in endless jealousy
from a distance but I don't
deserve you and you deserve so

much more than me.

You deserve a love that has

space for the man you were

created to be.

With me, I steal the best parts

of you.

You give it all to build our world.

You have been since the day you

Kissed me in that dim lit bar.

But you never believed me.

You shouldn't wonder.

You should believe and know.

Let me go.

For you and me.

K. Fortis

For You

Breathe Again

Life isn't always roses and

rainbows...

For You

LOVE HURTS

"Your Girl Is Lovely Hubble"

Tears are rolling down my face

and the breathing is going out

deeper than I can get back in.

I see your name across my phone.

Your words, generic as ever, are

cutting straight through me.

What the fuck did you decide to

ruin me?

Just because you were broken?

It has always been because of

your brokenness.

It was never because of me.

I can still feel the way you

looked at me from across that

booth in our bar.

You meant every word you said, "I

don't want anything more with

you. You have responsibility I'm

not ready to take on."

God! You were right.

The one and only honest thing

you ever said to me.

I should've kissed your forehead

and said, "you're beautiful" and

walked away, for good, right

then.

We were everything....

Everything never meant to last.

Dreams Come True

I dreamt of you last night.

I was swiping through photos and then suddenly I saw you.

You were standing there with a smile that didn't look quite like the you I know.

Your arms around a girl in a posed prom hold.

The caption read... a little formal for a 3rd date but

practicing for our future.

It ripped my soul out.

Lashed and laid out on the
table. I woke up in a panic,
hoping that it was in some way,
the universe waking me up to see
a message from you.

Sweating and in complete
desperation opened every form of
possible communication.

Nothing.

Maybe you've really let go this time.

The universe and my dreams agreed.

Full Moons & Rehab

You checked into rehab yesterday

and I died tonight.

It's a full moon.

Of course it is, as you would say.

Here's to you babe.

A whiskey down and maybe I'll

meet you there because full

moons and tequila and target

and love.

I found out you weren't dead

today but then I died a little

more inside.

Dear You

How are you today?

I'm ok.

Better than yesterday....

A little.

It's strange isn't it?

The way you have a tendency to

make the movies real.

I guess you're not a singer and

I'm not your wife but near death

rehab feels all too familiar.

Your family is scrambling for

answers and solutions.

I didn't want to tell them there

aren't any.

That you can't force someone to

want more.

I'm not sure your dad could

handle the same truth you put

me through.

I can't tell him what it felt like

to hear how content you were

with complacency.

How's the food in there?

Are you making friends who will

understand you more than I

could?

I tried.

I hope they find your heart and

soul there.

The one I love.

The one I don't think I'll ever be

allowed to see again.

Please, if I can ask just one
last thing of you,
Stay alive.
I don't know how I'm going to
survive without you in my life
but I know, for certain, that I
won't survive if you aren't still
walking this earth.
Love, Me

Oh Gene

You're within me.

I try.

Gene, I'm trying.... So hard.

I'm reading all the fucking

books.

I'm going to therapy.

I'm doing the work.

But you're still here.

Maybe you transformed me.

Maybe I'm trapped now in the

cycle.

Maybe I now need the 12 steps.

I need to find this separation.

But I don't want to.

I'm not ready to give you up.

To live this life without you.

I literally know less than nothing

about you.

Maybe you're here....

Maybe you're gone but I don't

think you are.

Maybe I just don't want you to

be.

I can't define the difference any

more.

I'm destroyed....

Are you?!

I'm surrounded by lies and that

should feel familiar but it's not.

Please watch season 5 Kayla

Kupono Addiction dance from So

You Think You Can Dance.

I know it's exactly what you

don't need.

Exactly what you're growing

away from.

Maybe you've become bigger than

that now.

But I'm trapped here.

At the end of the day.

Here I am...

Unable to leave in case you

return.

La La Land

Isn't it ironic that we were in

La La Land

to watch this magical musical

premiere

without knowing we were about

to see ourselves

on the big screen.

Living in the purple glow

and not being able to find a

way to make it work.

Uncage Me

You only love me because I am
the best me when I am flying
free.

The best me is the uncaged
version of myself.

I make you believe in yourself
and you know that I already
know your highest potential and
how completely possible it is to
achieve it.

Zero expectations and

unconditional love comes easily

when I don't belong to you.

I know you want to pick this

wild flower and keep me

somewhere to admire.

For your own.

Not letting anyone else too close

because I am yours.

But I fade into a shriveled dead

version of myself.

If anything is true about life is
that you can't have it all.

A lesson I still haven't learned.

This might be the most
hypocritical thing I've ever put on
paper but the truth hurts, even
for the messenger.

I want to need you.

I want to be captured.

Picked.

Saved.

Yet I can't be.

The only way to truly have me,

is not to, at all.

To get the me you love and need,

you have to live without me.

You have to let me come in and

out as I please.

No promises or compromises or

commitments.

Don't stop loving me but I know

you'll have to leave this life one

day.

Most souls need to settle.

Maybe one day mine will too.

Until then I'll let the wind toss

me around and leave my petals

scattered.

K. Fortis

For You

MISS YOU

The Last Time

I'm not sure why but I can't remember the last time I saw you.

It feels like years ago and I'm sure it wasn't.

But was it good?

Was it bad?

I can't remember if we drank or laughed.

My mind feels foggy about you.

I remember thinking I couldn't get

you a Christmas present.

And then I got your card.

But those are all the pieces I

remember.

I can't forget you yet.

I can't be wiping you out so fast.

But for some reason, I can't

remember the last time.

Maybe because I didn't know it

was going to be the last time.

This Too Shall Pass

Days are short but the weeks

are long and I can't tell if it's

been forever or just a moment.

I'm not really heartbroken

anymore, most days.

What are the 7 stages of grief?

I feel like Sooki.

I stopped counting them after the

one about tequila.

See, look, I'm funny, again, now.

You write to my husband as

though you still believe to your

core that you are some kind

of hero and my cousin writes to

make sure your mom is ok.

My heart stops for a second

and then it revives itself as

though mini imaginary heart

attacks are a legitimate reality

now.

I drink and think about how

"you never will again, because

you just can't now" and cheers

you in my mind.

Oh fucking hell, to sound British

because you loved my accents.

Who really cares though, since

you've blocked only me....

Everyone else I love, you've

decided to Keep an open line for.

FucK me, I guess, for being the

one who helped, and cared, and

loved you.

For being broken and hurt and needing more than a lazy, alcoholic, creative who refused to be present in any moment of his life.

Anyways, let me sip another sip and sleep in a little later tomorrow so that I can wake up refreshed after all this.

This too shall pass.

Lifetimes

Can you imagine if it took me years to get over him how many lifetimes it'll take me to get over you?

Reality is Rough

I miss you so fucking much right now.

My heart is slowly breaking all over again it seems.

Like I hadn't already moved forward.

I thought I was better but I can help but wonder where you are.

What you're doing.

How you're surviving this or if

you're thriving in it.

I miss the romance and I'm

finally allowing myself to cry

about it for the first time in a

month.

I miss being loved and kissed and

touched

and helped and romanced.

I miss being in love.

I miss wanting someone with my

whole heart.

I want to be ok.

I want to focus on life and use

this time for me. Instead I just

can't seem to be ok.

I was really sick last week and

asleep for 2 days.

I can't believe you don't care to

know how I am.

I want to think it impossible for

you to not be checking up on me.

But I guess that's reality now.

I fucking hate reality now.

1881

Flashbacks are heavy right now.

I know eventually they will

disappear into the abyss in my

mind.

Along with all the others.

Memories I have to tug hard to

pull back to the surface.

But today...

Here on the road.

They are in full force and

dancing in bars after 4 too

many.

I can smell it and remember

how it felt to laugh while

watching that tv above the bar.

To have our flasks and coffee

cups and sweating glasses from

the bar all on the same small

round top.

So today isn't a good day but

maybe tomorrow will be better.

Maybe tomorrow the silence I've surrounded myself with won't be filled with visions of us.

Wonder

I wonder if you wonder...

If you come on here to see if I'm

ok.

Knowing full well I'll never be.

I wonder what my new playlist

sounds like on your phone.

I wonder if it sounds like mine.

I wonder if you even wonder at

all or you're above the wondering.

I haven't been able to be above

it for more than a week at a

time and my god that is ducking

progress.

I actually have to auto correct

that now.

Funny how everything has

changed.

Even my smart phone knows it's

time for me to move on.

And still here I am....

backtracking and wondering.

So in case you happen to be wondering today...

I just added Time by NF and If the World Was Ending by JP Saxe.

Knowing that even here, at the end of the world, you still have that full fantasy, absolutely not my reality, effect on my life.

So I was just wondering if you still wonder.

Unturned Stones

Such a strange feeling tonight.

I drove all the way to the top of

Lake Avenue.

Why didn't we ever do that

before?

How is it possible we left stones

unturned?

I'm driving with a sip and a

burn.

The flowers are starting to go to

sleep.

But the sun is far too bright for

it to be our hour, just yet.

Purple hour monster, I miss you.

I should've prefaced this with the

fact that Sober by Demi Lovato

is what's playing at this exact

moment in time.

This moment that is already

becoming my past.

The way you have always been.

I guess I just thought you'd

always be my future too.

Today has had a slow burn.

The tears swelled out of nowhere

while I sat at my desk tonight.

As she sang, Is That Alright?

I felt you again for the first

time in a long time.

But it's all just different now.

Wish

I know it could never be but God
I wish.

I wish it was you.

I wish you could be the one

meeting my friends.

Road tripping with me.

Sippin whiskey.

Laughing our asses off.

Talking about our one of a kind

movie romance.

I wish it was you.

Boiling Point

Drink to the point of lifelessness.

Now my body can be in tune

with my mind.

It hurts until I'm so numb I can

no longer move.

The only thing I can't control

now are these tears.

They just fall as though the

boiling over from deep within me

has risen to my eyes.

It has completely consumed every ounce of me.

I can't breath now unless you answer.

Just a simple hello would bring me back to life.

I cry harder in disbelief as the phone just rings on.

Is it possible that you don't wonder?

That you don't worry?

That you no longer care?

Is this really.... it?

It Hurts

It hurts to be alive today.

Hurts to not hear your voice.

Hurts to not have you to cheer

me up.

Hurts that I'm doing the work

and I still can't have you.

Hurts to know that I'm lost here

without you.

I know I can survive.

I know I can thrive.

I started a business.

A new car.

A new puppy.

A whole life and yet...

It hurts to breathe.

Are you completely ok without

me?

It hurts to be alive today.

You Wrote

"I'm still connected to you on those different planes across different universes.", you wrote.

You wrote after the crash and fall and before the total silence.

You wrote before I had completely dismantled and before my heart became un-numb.

You wrote before I came out of complete shock.

You wrote before you found some
kind of sanity without me.

You wrote from a place I've
never known or seen within you.

You wrote before I realized I
can't do this life without you.

You wrote and I cried and you
never knew.

You wrote without knowing what
had happened out here without
you.

You wrote before I knew memories

weren't as erasable as pictures

and texts.

You wrote a lifetime ago....

And I hope it's still true.

It's Different Now

Are you the same as you've

always been?

Or is everything different now?

Have you changed not only your

routines and where you live but

who you are?

Have you written more?

You were always better at

writing stories when I wasn't

around.

You were always better at life without me around.

And me....

I've always been terrible at life either way.

I lost me somewhere along the ride and never fully recovered.

Dig deep, they say.

So I dig deeper and deeper and come up winded and more disoriented than I went under.

Music is the only thing that feels

like me, so I turn it off.

Because the only thing I find

within me, is you.

So I guess I'm the same as I've

always been.

You're Everywhere

Always, constantly around me.

In the whispering of wild plants

and sunsets.

In almost every song that plays

on the radio.

You surround me in the purple

hues of the sky and all my

assumptions of your new pass

times.

I live for the times you might be

driving right by me or in the

possibility of the future.

In every travel plan I make and

within every word that passes

through my mind.

In every moment of silence I

know you would fill.

In the moments I want to be my

silliest self.

And when I'm desperately

deprived of infatuation.

You surround me all ways,

always.

Give Up

I think I'd give up drinking for
you.

The idea of being drunk on your
love sounds better than any high
I've had in the last 6 months.

Let me drink you in.

Lick my lips after your kiss to
take in every last drop of that
lust.

I want to sleep in for hours

after spending all hours of the

night exploring this new you.

Dreaming as our new reality.

I know everything it could be.

But a part of me doesn't think

you'd want that.

Or me.

Without the haze of the drink

you'd see me clearly and realized

you never loved me at all.

But I.... I'd give up drinking for

you.

For You

SELF LOVE

Affirmations

Everything happens for a reason.

I will be happy.

I will get happier.

I will have my barn.

I will live my best life.

I will get healthy.

I am beautiful.

I am a great mom.

I will be loved.

Expectations

I sit here, overlooking a park, in

love with this paper and pen.

This truth.

This raw, brutal honesty.

These lines that don't know how

to lie and hold these truths

forever.

He said "Let me make my

intentions clear..."

Yet, I feel so unsure of what they

are.

Maybe my confusion is self inflicted.

Maybe I am choosing to misunderstand his simple words.

He "likes" me....

He wants to "date" me...

My expectations become greater with each second longer on this ground I stand upon.

I want...

I need....

So many unreasonable things.

Things I can't even live up to.

I want plans, and family, and

all the hours in a day, and

sacrifice, and honesty, and

undivided attention, and heart,

and soul, and passion, and

romance, and gentle intimacy,

and fire.

I want to be Johnny & June and

Big & Carrie.

I want love songs and romance novels and movies.

Dance with me in hallways, and spin me around with every hug.

Learn the way I drink my coffee.

Send me sweet messages every chance you get.

Make me feel like the only girl in your life.

Learn my day to day.

Aspire to make my dreams

reality.

Be wonderful even when we hate

each other.

Never let me fall asleep without

your arms around me.

Hug me even when I seem too

strong and don't let go or ask

me why I'm crying when I fall

into you.

Sometimes I need you to be the strong one.

Speak to me for hours about the things we can't change.

Make me feel like the smartest, most courageous woman you know.

This list is endless and so complex.

But if you can make me scream in your speeding car, I

can make you feel like a King.

I can and will do everything and more than you ever knew you needed or wanted.

I will pleasure you and give you myself in all the ways you've ever wanted.

I will be your defender and hold your name high.

I will make sure you know how much you mean to me daily and

how no one else will ever

compare.

Nor have the chance to try.

My expectations are high.... But I

will make yours higher.

Fuck This Song

Weird going through my playlist today.

It's all you.

I have been the one drowning myself in you for the last 6 years.

All along I believed it was you holding me down but the truth is I wasn't fighting my way back up.

Here's the proof.

Singing me back into sadness.

I can see that dance on the beach you spoke of long ago.

It just looks slightly differently now.

Definitely romantic in all its beauty but truth over shadows it.

The truth that all that was ever good about us was the

fantasy.

The fantasy you never intended

to live up to.

The dream that you knew to

your core was a nightmare.

I just didn't believe you in your

truth.

In every realization you had,

telling me you were the devil, I

fantasized about it and the

way you wanted to control me.

I completely missed the part
where, all you were was the
temptation and misdirection to
capture me in hell with you.

You needed people to take some
of the flames.

To hold some of the heat.

You knew there was no flying
through the stars.

You knew other universes didn't
exist.

And if you didn't and you

believed this to your core, I know

you wouldn't have jumped without

my hand in yours.

I'm growing now though.

Tears aren't falling as I write

this.

For the first time ever, I can see

clearly and hear this song and

think of me and how romantic I

am and that has nothing

to do with you.

As I have nothing to do with

your drowning and suffering and

I never did.

This Is It

This is it.

The moment I change again.

Broken or not.

I lose all the pieces of me.

The parts you knew in detail.

The old me is gone now.

You can have her.

She will forever belong to you.

I can't deal with being her for

one more second.

This is it.

K. Fortis

For You

Finale

Drum roll please...

For You

,

A letter to me,

I'm coming for you.
To collect every last piece of
me.
I'm sorry I left you behind.
Having to relive that day
over and over...
I'm so sorry.
I know it feels like the only
life you've ever known.
And God I know that there's
safety in familiarity.
But it's false, my dear.
The happiness relived again
and again, but it's not real,
my love.
It's destroying you from the
inside out.
It's a slow rot.
The truth is that it's feeding
on you.

Every time you awake in
the same place it takes
another sip from your soul.
And a little more of you is
lost.
But I promise it's not forever.
I'm here to save you.
I'm coming for you.
In all my weakness.
I'm picking up what's left of
myself and coming for you.
Together we will be stronger
and maybe one day, even
complete.
So let go, even in fear, but
let go of that now and come
with me.
I promise I'll protect you, now.
I can promise you that, at
least.
It won't be easy and it's

going to hurt but at the very
least you'll be alive and in
the light and living in truth.
So I'm coming for you now.

Love,
Yourself

Letter to my reader,

 I hope you've enjoyed this journey of love, passion, destruction, and codependency. I've left you a few pages to find your inner muse. I'm sending you all the love in the world for giving me this chance to find a place within your hearts.

 Love You,

 Krystel Fortis

NOTES

_____

_____

_____

_____

_____

_____

_____

_____

_____

_____

NOTES

NOTES

_____

_____

_____

_____

_____

_____

_____

_____

_____

_____

_____

NOTES

_____

_____

_____

_____

_____

_____

_____

_____

_____

_____

_____

_____

NOTES

NOTES

K. Fortis

For You

CPSIA information can be obtained
at www.ICGtesting.com
Printed in the USA
LVHW010151010820
662091LV00011B/767